SHARKS

Anna Claybourne
Consultant: Trevor Day

BYEWAY
BOOKS

First published in 2005 by Miles Kelly Publishing Ltd
Bardfield Centre, Great Bardfield
Essex, CM7 4SL

This 2005 edition published by Byeway Books
Byeway Books Inc.
Lenexa, KS 66219, 866-4BYEWAY
www.byewaybooks.com

Editorial Director: Belinda Gallagher

Editorial Assistant: Hannah Todd

Designer: Tom Slemmings

Picture Researcher: Liberty Newton

Production: Estela Boulton, Elizabeth Brunwin

Library of Congress Cataloging-in-Publication Data
is on file at the Library of Congress.

ISBN 1-933581-07-7

Printed in China

2 4 6 8 10 9 7 5 3 1

The publishers would like to thank the following artists who have contributed to this book:
John Butler, Jim Channel, Luigi Galante, Colin Howard (Advocate Art), Andrea Morandi,
Mike Saunders, Rudi Vizi, Mike White (Temple Rogers)

All other pictures are from MKP Archives, Corel, digitalvision, Hemera

Contents

All about sharks 4

Shark sizes 6

Inside a shark 8

Shark skin 10

Tails and fins 12

How sharks breathe 14

How sharks swim 16

Sensing smells 18

Shark vision 20

The sixth sense 22

What sharks eat 24

How sharks hunt 26

Meeting and mating 28

Shark eggs 30

Growing up 32

Where sharks live 34

Sharks and humans 36

Endangered species 38

Index 40

All about sharks

- **Sharks are a type of fish**. They live and breathe underwater and are brilliant swimmers.

- **All sharks are carnivores,** which means they eat other animals. Many are fierce hunters.

- **Sharks are found** in seas and oceans and in a few rivers too.

- **There are about** 400 different species of shark.

- **A species is the name** for a particular type of shark or other living thing. Sharks of the same species can mate and have young, which also belong to that species.

- **Most sharks** have long bodies, triangle-shaped fins and lots of sharp teeth.

- **Sharks range in size** from about the size of a banana to bigger than a bus.

- **Sharks are closely related** to other fish called rays and skates. They are similar to sharks but usually have much flatter bodies.

- **Sharks have existed** for almost 400 million years.

- **Most sharks** are not dangerous. Only a few species have been known to attack humans.

▶ *A great white shark on the prowl among a shoal of fish. Many sharks hunt and eat other types of fish, as well as all kinds of sea creatures.*

Shark sizes

- **The whale shark** is the biggest living shark. It can reach a maximum size of 60 ft (18 m)—as long as two buses end-to-end.

- **The biggest shark ever**, *Megalodon*, is now extinct. Scientists think it may have weighed almost twice as much a whale shark.

- **The biggest sharks** are gentle creatures that filter tiny food particles from the water.

- **The biggest hunting shark** is the great white shark.

- **A great white shark's mouth** can measure 16 in (40 cm) across.

- **Most sharks are medium-sized**, measuring between 3 ft and 10 ft (1 m and 3 m) in length.

- **The smallest sharks** are the spined pygmy shark and the dwarf lanternshark. They would fit on two pages of this book.
- **The average size for a shark** is very similar to the size of a human.
- **Although some sharks** are small, most are bigger than other types of fish.
- **Sharks aren't the biggest animals** in the ocean. Some whales are bigger— but they are mammals, not fish.

▼ *This is a whale shark, the biggest shark of all. It swims along with its mouth wide open in order to collect food from the water.*

Inside a shark

- **Sharks are vertebrates**, which means they have a skeleton with a backbone. Many types of animals, including all fish, reptiles, birds, and mammals, are vertebrates.

- **Sharks' skeletons** are not made of bone, but of cartilage.

- **If you cut a shark open**, you'd find a thick layer of muscles just under its skin. The shark uses them to move its body from side to side as it swims along.

- **A shark's vital organs** are mostly in a cavity in the middle of its body. Sharks have many of the same organs as humans and other animals, including a stomach, liver, and kidneys.

- **Sharks have** extra-large livers that contain a lot of oil. As oil is lighter than water, this helps it to float.

- **A shark's stomach** is very stretchy. It can expand so that the shark can consume a large amount of food in a short space of time.

- **Just like humans**, sharks have a heart that pumps blood around their bodies.

- **Most sharks** are cold-blooded, which means their blood is the same temperature as the water around them.

- **A few sharks**, such as mako and thresher sharks, are warm-blooded— they can heat their blood up so that they are warmer than their surroundings. This helps them to swim faster and move into colder areas of the ocean to hunt.

▼ *Some of the main organs and other body parts of a shark's body.*

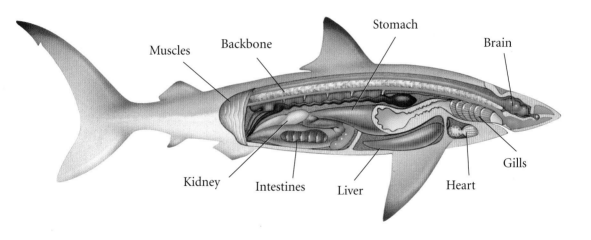

Stomach

Muscles

Backbone

Brain

Kidney

Intestines

Liver

Heart

Gills

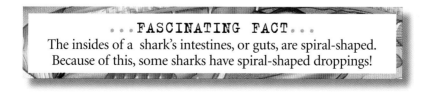

...FASCINATING FACT...
The insides of a shark's intestines, or guts, are spiral-shaped.
Because of this, some sharks have spiral-shaped droppings!

Shark skin

- **Sharks don't have scales**, like other fish. Instead their skin is covered with tiny, hard points called denticles.

- **The word "denticle"** means "little tooth"—because denticles are very similar to teeth.

- **Denticles make a shark's skin** feel very rough to the touch. Some swimmers have been badly scratched just from brushing against a shark.

- **Denticles have two uses:** they protect the shark from enemies and help it to slide through the water.

- **Denticles range** from microscopic in size to about 0.2 in (5 mm) across.

▼ *Along with its streamlined shape the denticles on a shark's skin helps it to slide smoothly through the water.*

◀ *A close-up of a Greenland shark's denticles. On this part of the shark's body, the denticles are all pointing in the same direction to help water flow that way.*

● **The shape of denticles** varies on different parts of a shark's body, and from one shark species to another.

● **Denticles on the side** of a shark are the sharpest—ensuring fast movement through the water.

● **Sharks also release** a slimy substance from their skin, to make their bodies move through the water even faster.

● **Large sharks have very thick skin**—thicker than a human finger.

> ...FASCINATING FACT...
> Shark skin is so rough that in the past it was used to make a type of sandpaper, called shagreen.

Tails and fins

- **A typical shark** has up to seven fins, not including its tail.

- **The big fin** on a shark's back is called the dorsal fin. It's the one that can be seen sticking out of the water in shark films and cartoons.

- **A shark's tail** is also known as its "caudal fin."

- **A shark's tail is made up** of two points called lobes—an upper lobe and a lower lobe.

- **There are two large pectoral** fins near the front of a shark's body, a bit like arms. The shark uses them steer while swimming.

- **Epaulette sharks** use their pectoral fins like legs to "crawl" along the sea bed.

- **In parts of Asia,** people use sharks' fins to make a special kind of soup.

- **Thresher sharks** can be recognized by their very long upper tail lobes.

- **A whale shark's pectoral fin** can be 6 ft (2 m) long—that's as big as a bed!

Dorsal fin

▲ *Hammerhead sharks have very long dorsal fins*

▶ *A shark turns, clearly showing its long pectoral fins.*

...FASCINATING FACT...

Without their fins, sharks wouldn't be able to stay the right way up. They'd roll over in the water.

How sharks breathe

◀ *A silky shark. All five gill slits on the side of the shark's throat can be clearly seen.*

- **Like most animals**, sharks need to take in oxygen to make their bodies work.

- **Like other fish**, sharks breathe underwater using gills in their throats.

- **Most sharks have five pairs of gills**. Each gill is made up of a set of feathery, hair-like filaments full of blood vessels.

- **Many sharks** have extra breathing holes called spiracles, just behind their eyes, that take in water for the shark to breathe.

- **As a shark swims**, water flows into its mouth or spiracles, and past the gills. They take oxygen out of the water and carry it into the shark's bloodstream.

- **The water flows out again** through the gill slits—the lines you can see on the sides of a shark's neck.

- **Sharks don't have lungs**—their gills do the same job that lungs do in humans.

- **Some fast sharks**, such as mako sharks, have to keep swimming in order to keep breathing. If they stop, water stops flowing past their gills and they suffocate.

- **Slow-moving sharks** such as the Port Jackson shark can pump water across their gills, so they can stop for a rest and still keep breathing.

> ...FASCINATING FACT...
> Seawater contains just one percent oxygen gas—
> much less than air, which is 21 percent oxygen.

How sharks swim

▶ White-tip reef sharks often stop
swimming to rest on the sea bed.
As they are heavier than water,
they have to start swimming
again if they want to move
off the sea bed.

● **A shark's main
  swimming organ**
  is its tail. The shark
  thrashes it from side
  to side to push itself
  through the water.

● **Sharks use their pectoral** and
  pelvic fins to help them steer
  and swim upward and downward.

● **The fastest shark** is the shortfin mako shark, which has been recorded
  swimming at over 19 mph (30 km/h).

● **Most sharks have** an everyday cruising speed of around 5 mph (8km/h).

● **Sharks normally swim** with a relaxed, regular rhythm. They don't dart
  around like most bony fish do.

```
...FASCINATING FACT...
If sharks don't keep swimming, they
gradually sink onto the sea bed.
```

- **Other bony fish** have a swim bladder—a gas-filled organ that keeps them afloat. But sharks don't have swim bladders, so they are slightly heavier than water.

- **Many sharks swim** in a figure-of-eight pattern when they are annoyed.

- **Thanks to their streamlined shape**, sharks can swim very quietly and sneak up on their prey.

- **Some sharks swallow air** to help them to float better.

▼ *A shark's torpedo-shaped body makes it a very fast swimmer.*

Sensing smells

- **The sense of smell** is the most important sense for most sharks.

- **As a shark swims**, water constantly flows into the nostrils on its snout, and over the scent-detecting cells inside them.

- **Sharks can smell blood** in water, even if it's diluted to one part in ten million. That's like one drop of blood mixed into a small swimming pool.

- **A shark can smell** an injured animal up to half a mile away.

- **The biggest part** of a shark's brain is the olfactory lobe—the part used for processing smells.

- **The great white shark** has biggest olfactory lobe of all—which means it probably has the best sense of smell of any shark.

- **Swimmers have been known** to attract sharks just by having a tiny scratch on their skin.

- **Sharks use their nostrils** for smelling, not breathing.

- **A shark homes in on a scent** by zig-zagging its snout from side to side. It moves toward the side where the smell is strongest.

> ...FASCINATING FACT...
> In one experiment, a scientist plugged one of a shark's nostrils. It swam around in a circle!

▶ *A great white shark hunting, trying to detect traces of blood from injured fish or other animals. The water flows into the nostrils at the front of its snout as it swims along.*

Shark vision

▲ *When hunting, sharks such as this great white use their eyesight to help them close in accurately on their prey.*

- **Most sharks have big eyes** and good eyesight. They mainly use it to spot their prey.

- **Sharks need** to be able to see well in the dark—as there is limited light underwater.

- **Many sharks** have a shiny layer called the *tapetum lucidum* at the back of their eyes. It collects and reflects light, helping them to see, even in the gloomy darkness.

- **The *Tapetum lucidum*** (which is Latin for "bright carpet") makes sharks' eyes appear to glow in the dark.

- **Some sharks** have slit-shaped pupils, like a cat's.

● **Scientists think** sharks can probably see in color, like humans.

● **Some very deepwater sharks** have small eyes and poor eyesight. That's because the deepest oceans are so dark, many animals living there rely on other senses instead.

● **Sharks have a third eye**, called a pineal eye, under the skin in their foreheads. It can't see properly like a normal eye, but it can sense daylight.

● **The shy-eye shark** gets its name because when it is caught, it covers its eyes with its tail to shield them from the light.

▲ *A close-up of a tiger shark's eye, showing a special eyelid called the nictitating membrane. This closes over the eye when the shark is about to bite, to protect it from being damaged in a struggle.*

...FASCINATING FACT...
Most sharks never close their eyes. Some have special see-through eyelids that protect their eyes without cutting out any light. Others just roll their eyes up into their head to protect them.

The sixth sense

▼ *The ampullae of Lorenzini scattered across a shark's snout can be seen clearly here. Each ampulla looks like a tiny hole or pit. Under the surface of the skin, it opens out into a wider bottle shape, containing a jelly that collects electrical signals.*

- **A shark has six senses**. Besides having vision, hearing, touch, taste, and smell, sharks can also sense the small amounts of electricity given off by other animals.

- **To detect electricity**, a shark has tiny holes in the skin around its head and snout. They're called the "ampullae of Lorenzini."

- **Ampullae** are a type of Roman bottle. The ampullae of Lorenzini get their name because of their narrow-necked bottle shape.

- **Each ampulla** contains a jelly-like substance that collects electric signals.

- **All animals** give off tiny amounts of electricity when their muscles move. Electricity doesn't travel well through air, but it travels well through water.

- **A shark's ampullae of Lorenzini** can sense animals within a range of about 3 ft (1 m).

- **Some sharks** use their electrical sense to find prey that's buried in the sea bed.

- **A fierce hunting shark**, such as a tiger or hammerhead, has up to 1,500 ampullae of Lorenzini.

- **Stefano Lorenzini** was an Italian anatomist (body scientist). He studied the ampullae of Lorenzini, and gave them their name, in 1678.

> ...FASCINATING FACT...
> Some other animals can detect electricity
> too—including the duck-billed platypus.

What sharks eat

- **Most sharks eat** many different kinds of animals.

- **Big, fast hunting sharks**, such as great whites and bull sharks, feed on large fish (including other sharks), as well as seals, turtles, octopuses, squid, seabirds, and other sea creatures.

- **Many smaller sharks**, such as dogfish sharks, hunt smaller fish, octopuses, and squid.

- **Slow-moving sharks**, such as nurse sharks, angel sharks, and carpet sharks, crunch up crabs, shrimps, and shellfish that they find on the sea bed.

- **Filter-feeders** are sharks that feed on plankton, tiny floating animals and plants, which they filter out of the water.

- **There are hardly any** animal species in the ocean that aren't part of the diet of one shark or another.

- **Tiger sharks** are well-known for eating anything they can find, including objects that aren't food, such as tin cans.

- **After being eaten**, food stays in a shark's stomach for up to three days.

- **Most sharks don't eat every day.** Some big hunters can go without food for months.

...FASCINATING FACT...
Sharks generally prefer the taste of fish,
seals, and turtles to the taste of humans.

▲ *Hammerhead sharks prey on other sharks, rays, bony fish, crabs and lobsters, octopuses, and squid.*

How sharks hunt

- **Most sharks are nocturnal**—which means they hunt at night—or crepuscular—which means they hunt at dusk.

- **Before attacking**, some sharks "bump" their prey with their snouts, probably to see if it's something edible and tasty.

- **When about to bite**, a shark raises its snout and thrusts its jaws forward, so that its teeth stick out to grab the prey.

- **Some sharks shake their prey** from side to side to rip it apart.

- **Sharks don't usually chew**, they tear their prey into chunks or just swallow it whole.

- **Sharks can attack** animals much bigger than themselves. For example, great whites have been known to bite chunks out of whales.

- **Sometimes**, lots of sharks are attracted to a source of food, and they all jostle to eat it at the same time. This is known as a "feeding frenzy."

- **Most hunting sharks** prefer prey that's weak or helpless, because it's easier to catch. That's why sharks are good at smelling blood; it tells them when an animal is injured.

- **Many sharks give their prey** a fatal bite, then leave it to bleed to death. They then return to feed on the body.

> ...FASCINATING FACT...
> Sharks have very strong jaws. They can bite other animals in half—even those with tough shell, such as turtles.

▼ *This great white shark is about to take a bite out of a piece of meat dangled from a boat. Although it's not hunting, you can see how it lifts its snout up high and thrusts its teeth forward to attack.*

Meeting and mating

◀ *Male white-tip reef sharks sometimes spend time resting in shallow water during the day. If they smell a pheromone scent from a female telling them she's looking for a mate, they will try to find her.*

- **Like most animals**, sharks have to mate in order to reproduce.

- **Mating happens** when a male and a female of the same species meet up, and the male gives the female some cells from his body. This allows her to make new young inside her body.

- **Nurse sharks**, blue sharks, and many other species have special mating areas in shallow parts of the ocean.

- **In other species**, such as white-tip reef sharks, the females release pheromones to help the males find them.

- **Male sharks sometimes bite** female sharks to show they want to mate with them.

- **Female sharks** often have thicker skin than males so that being bitten during courtship doesn't harm them.

- **When sharks mate**, the male uses two body parts called claspers to deliver cells into an opening in the female's body, called the cloaca.

- **Sharks often wind their bodies** around each other when they are mating.

- **Sharks don't mate very often**. In most species, they reproduce only once every two years.

> ... FASCINATING FACT ...
> The ancient Greek scientist and writer Aristotle studied and
> wrote about how sharks mate over 2,300 years ago.

Shark eggs

- **Many sharks have young** by laying eggs, as most bony fish do. Sharks that do this are called "oviparous" sharks.

- **Bullhead**, dogfish, horn, zebra, and swell sharks are all oviparous sharks.

- **A typical shark** lays between 10 and 20 eggs at a time.

- **A mother shark** doesn't guard her eggs. She lays them in a safe place, such as between two rocks or under a clump of seaweed, then leaves them to hatch.

- **Sharks' eggs** are enclosed in protective eggcases. The egg cases come in many shapes, including tubes, spirals, and pillow shapes.

- **When the female** first lays her eggs, their cases are soft, but when they come in contact with the seawater, they get harder.

- **Like a chicken's egg**, a shark egg contains a yolk that feeds the baby as it grows bigger.

- **Inside the egg**, a shark baby grows for between six and ten months before hatching.

- **You can sometimes find empty** shark eggcases washed up on beaches. They're known as "mermaid's purses."

▶ *A fully-formed Port Jackson shark emerges from its spiral-shaped egg case.*

...FASCINATING FACT...
Catsharks' eggs have sticky strings on them that wind
around seaweed, holding the eggs secure.

▲ *A mother Port Jackson shark laying an egg. After laying, female Port Jackson sharks pick up their eggcases in their mouths and wedge them into a safe place, such as between two rocks.*

31

Growing up

- **Sharks grow slowly**. It can take a pup up to 20 years to grow into an adult.

- **Blue sharks** are among the fastest growers. A blue shark pup grows about 1 ft (30 cm) longer every year, changing from a 2 in (50 cm) long pup to an adult up to 13 ft (4 m) long.

- **As shark pups are small**, predators often try to eat them. The biggest danger comes from other adult sharks that prey on any type of smaller fish. Sometimes, pups even get eaten by adults of their own species.

- **For every ten shark pups** born, only one or two will survive to be adults.

- **Many types of shark pups** live in "nursery areas"— shallow parts of the ocean close to the shore, where there are plenty of hiding places to shelter in and smaller sea creatures to feed on.

▲ *As a baby shark develops, it feeds on the yolk from its egg. This is a lanternshark pup with its yolk.*

...FASCINATING FACT...
Even when they reach adulthood, sharks don't stop growing. They just grow more slowly.

- **Sharks are born** with a full set of teeth (see shark teeth), so they can start hunting for their own food right away. Unlike the young of birds, humans, dogs, and cats, shark pups are never fed by their parents.

- **Young sharks** eat things such as small fish, shrimps, and baby octopuses. As sharks grow bigger, they hunt bigger prey.

- **A typical shark** lives for around 25 to 30 years, although some species, including whale sharks and dogfish sharks, may live for 100 years or more.

- **When a shark dies**, scientists can tell how old it is by counting growth rings in its spine—like the rings inside tree trunks.

▼ *Once a large shark, such as this great white, reaches adulthood, it is several yards long, and there are few other animals in the ocean that can harm it.*

Where sharks live

- **Sharks are found** in seas and oceans all around the world.

- **Sharks are almost all marine fish**—which means they live in the salty sea rather than in fresh water.

- **Just a few shark species** such as bull sharks and Ganges sharks can survive in fresh water, and swim out of the ocean into rivers and lakes.

- **Sharks are most common** around coasts. Many species like to live in shallow sandy bays, near coral reefs, or in the medium-deep water a few miles from the shore.

- **Coral reefs and seaweed forests** are an especially good home for young sharks. They provide them with food and hiding places.

- **Sharks that live out in the open ocean**, such as blue sharks, are known as pelagic sharks.

- **Many types of sharks**, such as wobbegongs, spend most of their time on the ocean floor. They're called benthic sharks.

- **Many sharks prefer warm waters**, such as those around Africa, Australia, Japan, and North and South America—but a few, such as the Greenland shark, live in cold water around the Arctic.

- **Sharks are hardly ever found** in the Southern Ocean around Antarctica— probably because it's too cold for them there.

> ...FASCINATING FACT...
> Epaulette sharks are often found in rock pools. They can move
> from one pool to another across dry land, by dragging
> themselves with their strong pectoral fins.

▼ *A scalloped hammerhead shark cruises across a coral reef—an underwater structure built by tiny creatures called coral polyps.*

Sharks and humans

- **Sharks have been around** for much longer than humans have.

- **It's a natural instinct** for people to be scared of sharks, as some of them are fierce hunters.

- **However**, people are more dangerous to sharks than the other way around.

- **Some sharks**, such as Greenland sharks and angel sharks, are among the easiest fish to catch with a hook or fishing spear, people have probably been eating them for thousands of years.

- **As well as for food**, people hunt sharks for all kinds of useful products such as sharkskin leather and liver oil (see more uses for sharks).

- **People in the Pacific islands** used shark teeth to make tools and weapons as long as 5,000 years ago.

- **In the 5th century** BC, the ancient Greek historian Herodotus wrote about how sharks attacked sailors when ships sank during battles at sea.

- **The ancient Greek** scientist Aristotle studied sharks in the 4th century BC, and was one of the first to notice that they were different in many ways from other fish.

- **Sharks are sometimes** described as cruel, heartless, vicious, or mean killers. In fact, like most meat-eating animals, sharks only kill in order to survive.

> **...FASCINATING FACT...**
> The word "shark" is sometimes used to
> mean a ruthless person or a thief.

▼ *Although people are scared of sharks, they are very interested in them too. This photographer is using an underwater camera to get the best possible close-up photo of a great white shark.*

Endangered species

- **An endangered species** is in danger of dying out and becoming extinct.

- **When a species becomes extinct**, all the members of that species die and it can never exist again.

- **Scientists try to find** out if a shark species is at risk by counting how many sharks are seen in a particular area and measuring how much this changes over time.

- **For example**, experts found that sandbar shark sightings on the east coast of the U.S.A. fell by 20 percent between the 1970s and the 1990s. The sandbar shark is now an endangered shark.

- **International organizations** such as the IUCN (International Union for the Conservation of Nature and Natural Resources) compile lists of which species are endangered.

- **According to the IUCN** over 50 shark species are now endangered.

- **Well-known sharks** that are endangered include great white, whale, and basking sharks.

- **Most sharks** have become endangered because of overfishing (see sharks in trouble).

- **Some sharks and shark relatives**, such as leopard sharks and sawfish, are threatened when natural coastlines and estuaries are developed and built on, for example to build tourist resorts. This destroys nursery areas where sharks lay eggs or bear their young.

- **The Ganges shark**, which is found in the river Ganges in India, is one of the most endangered sharks.

▲ *Great whites are one species that are known to be in danger of dying out. There are several international campaigns to try to save them.*

Index

Africa 34
age of sharks 33
air 19, 17
Americas 34
ampullae of Lorenzini 22, 23
anatomist, Lorenzini 23
anatomy, shark **8–9**
ancient Greeks 36
angel sharks 24, 36
Antarctica, sharks 34
Aristotle 29, 36
Australia 34

backbone 9
basking sharks 38
benthic sharks 34
biting 26, 27, 29
bladder, swim 17
blood 8 15, 18, 26
blue sharks 29, 32, 34
body shapes 4,
bonnethead sharks **5**
brain 9
breathing 4, **14–15**
bull sharks 24
bullhead shark 30

cannibalism 32
carnivore diet 4
carpet sharks 24
catsharks 31
caudal fin 12
chewing 26
claspers 29
cloaca 29
coastal sharks 34
cold-blooded 8
color vision 21
coral reefs 34, 35
courtship 29
crabs 24–25
crepuscular hunting 26

dangerous sharks 36
development 30, **32–33**
dogfish sharks 30, 33
dorsal fins 12
drag 11
duck-billed platypus 23
dwarf sharks 7

eating and prey **24–25**
eggs **30–31**, 30, 31
electricity detection **22–23**
endangered sharks **38–39**

epaulette shark 12, 34
extinction 6, 38
eyes and vision **20–21**, 20, 21

feeding 26
filter-feeding 6, 24
fins 4, **12–13**, 16. 34
fish 24–25, 33
foods **24–25**
freshwater sharks 34

Ganges shark 34, 38
gill 9, 14, 15
glow (bioluminescent) 20
great white sharks 6, 19, 26
    endangered 38, 39
    growth 33
    photographing 37
    prey 24
    vision 20
Greenland sharks 36, 34
growth **32–33**

habitat loss 38
Hammerhead shark 12, 23, 25
heart 8, 9
Herodotus 36
hornsharks 30
humans, and sharks **36–37**
hunting methods **26–27**

intelligence **27**
International Union for the
    Conservation of Nature
    and Natural Resources 38

Japan 34
jaws 26

kidney 8, 9

leather, skin 36
leopard shark 38
life span 33
light, sensing **20–21**
liver 8, 9
lobe, olfactory 18
lobes, of tail 12
lobsters 24–25
Lorenzini, ampullae of 22
Lorenzini, Stefano 23
lungs 15

mako sharks 8, 15, 29

mating **28–29**
Megalodon 6
mermaid's purse 30
muscles 8, 9, 23

nictitating membrane 21
nocturnal hunting 26
North America 34
nostrils 18, 19
nurse sharks 24, 29
nursery areas 32

octopuses 24–25, 33
oil, from liver 8, 36
olfactory lobe 18
organs, body 8, 9
origins 4
overfishing 38
oviparous 30
oxygen 15

parental care 33
pectoral fin 12, 13, 16, 34
photography 36
plankton 24
Port Jackson shark 15, 30, 31
prey **24–25**, 26
pupils, eye 20
pups 32–33
purse, mermaid's 30

rays 4
reef, coral 34
reproduction 29
rock pools 34
rolling, and fins 12, 13

sandbar shark 38
sandpaper 11
sawfish 38
scales, skin 10
scalloped hammerhead 35
scents, mating 29
scents, sensing **18–19**
scientific surveys 38
sea water, oxygen content 15
seabirds, as prey 24–25
seals 24–25
seaweed forests 34
senses **18–19**, **20–21**, 20, 21
shagreen 11
shaking prey 26
sharks
    and food **24–25**
    and humans **36–37**

as prey 24–25
    young 30
shrimps 24, 33
shy-eye shark 21
sight, sense of **20–21**, 20, 21
silky shark 14
sixth sense **22–23**
size 4, **6–7**
skates 4
skeleton 8
skin **10–11**, 29
South America, sharks 34
Southern Ocean, sharks 34
species 4
speed, swimming 16
spined pygmy shark 7
squid 24–25
steering 16
stomach 8, 9, 24
streamlined shape 17
survival, and killing 36
swallowing prey 26
swell shark 30
swimming **16–17**

tails **12–13**, 16
Tapetum lucidum 20
taste 24
teeth 10, 26, 27, 33
third eye 21
threatened species **38–39**
thresher sharks 12
tiger sharks 21, 23, 24
tools 36
tooth *see also* teeth 4
turtles 24–25 26

vertebrates 8
vision **20–21**, 20, 21

warm-blooded 8
warm-water species 34
weapons 36
whale sharks 12, 6–7, 33, 38
whales 7, 26
where sharks live **34–35**
white-tip reef shark 16, 28, 29
wobbegongs 34

yolk 30, 32
young sharks, growth 32–33

zebra sharks 30